Building the Union: reform of the institutions

THE INTERGOVERNMENTAL CONFERENCE OF THE EUROPEAN UNION 1996

Federal Trust Papers Number Three

Federal Trust Round Table

The Federal Trust has established a Round Table to discuss in depth the issues raised by the 1996 Intergovernmental Conference of the European Union, to monitor the processes of its preparation, negotiation and ratification, and to assess its outcome. A series of *Federal Trust Papers* is being published: the first, *State of the Union*, appeared in February 1995, and the second, *Towards the Single Currency* in May.

The Round Table is chaired by Lord Jenkins of Hillhead, President of the European Commission 1977-81; the rapporteur is John Pinder, Chairman of the Federal Trust; the secretary is Andrew Duff, Director of the Trust, to whom any written comments should be addressed.

The members of the Round Table, shown below, serve in an independent capacity and do not represent their organisations. They do not necessarily concur with all the opinions expressed in this *Federal Trust Paper*, but they support its general thrust and welcome it as a contribution to the debate about the future of the Union. The Federal Trust is an independent charity and, as such, holds no political view of its own.

Christopher Johnson
Charles Kennedy MP
Uwe Kitzinger
Christopher Layton
John Leech
Lord Lester QC
Jean-Victor Louis
Sarah Ludford
Peter Luff
Peter Mandelson MP
David Marquand
Andrew Marr
David Martin MEP
Richard Mayne
David Millar
Gary Miller
Frances Morrell
Edward Mortimer
Simon Nuttall
Sir Michael Palliser
Robin Pedler
John Pinder
Roy Pryce
Giles Radice MP
Paul Richards
Keith Richardson

Francesco Rossolillo
Malcolm Rutherford
Derek Scott
Michael Shackleton
Eleanor Sharpston
Baron Snoy d'Oppuers
John Stevens MEP
Susan Strange
Alastair Sutton
Susie Symes
Dick Taverne QC
Christopher Taylor
Anthony Teasdale
Lord Tugendhat
Sandy Walkington
Helen Wallace
WilliamWallace
Graham Watson MEP
Wolfgang Wessels
Martin Westlake
Richard Whitman
Shirley Williams
John Williamson
Ernest Wistrich
Stephen Woodard

Glossary

CAP	Common Agricultural Policy
CDU	Christian Democratic Union
CFSP	Common Foreign and Security Policy
CJHA	Cooperation in Justice and Home Affairs
CSU	Christian Social Union
EC	European Community
Ecu	European Currency Unit
EMI	European Monetary Institute
EMU	Economic and Monetary Union
EU	European Union
Gatt	General Agreement on Trade and Tariffs
IGC	Intergovernmental Conference
WEU	Western European Union

For the Citizen of Europe: a summary

The Intergovernmental Conference (IGC) to be convened in 1996 is to consider how to improve the European Union's institutions. The aim must be to ensure that the Union works to the fullest extent for the benefit of its citizens.

The institutions of the Community, and now the Union, have enabled it to make a great contribution to peace and prosperity. They have a unique capacity to deal with the consequences of growing interdependence among the member states. But the institutions must be made more effective and democratic in order to face the challenges ahead, particularly the enlargement to Central and Eastern Europe. The enlargement cannot succeed without such institutional reform.

Difficulties in ratifying the Maastricht Treaty were a warning against further extension of the Union's competences. The IGC should not seek to extend them. But we believe that reforms to improve the institutions will be welcomed by most of the Union's citizens, not least the British. We propose, for example, that the IGC should act to:

- strengthen the protection of fundamental rights and freedoms;

- open the legislative sessions of the Council to press and public;

- improve accountability of ministers to home parliaments;

- require all laws to be approved by the European Parliament as well as the Council;

- strengthen the control over agricultural spending by giving the Parliament equal powers with the Council, as for other budgetary expenditure;

- cut the number of Commissioners to a maximum of one from each member state;

- strengthen the powers to check fraud and lax financial control by member states in spending Union money and to punish those responsible;

- extend the jurisdiction of the Court of Justice so that citizens have recourse to judicial remedies with respect to any action by the Union's institutions.

These reforms would make the Union more open, democratic and effective. But it will not be effective enough without another reform that, even if not immediately popular, is necessary to enable the Union to work properly for the benefit of the citizens. With the number of member states soon to rise to twenty or more, the procedure of unanimity which gives each member state a veto in the Council becomes more and more impracticable. The IGC should confine that procedure to a minimum of Community matters of constitutional significance and enlarge the scope for majority voting in the field of foreign policy, security, justice and home affairs.

Reforms such as these would give the Union the capacity to build on the Community's achievements of prosperity and security, and to extend them to Europe as a whole. This is a vital interest of the British people and it is profoundly to be hoped that the British government will accept and promote such reforms.

If Britain or any other member state were to block the strengthening of the Union, a group led by France and Germany would be likely to intensify cooperation amongst themselves in order to guard against disintegration as the Union is enlarged. If this were to happen, those states that chose not to participate should cooperate in finding a way for core states to deepen their integration within, as far as possible, the Union's institutions, in order to limit the distance between the core group and the rest and to facilitate a subsequent rapprochement. A decision not to participate in such a group would seriously damage British interests.

Thus a constructive British approach to reform of the institutions is needed. The main aims should be to open up the Council and improve the accountability of the ministers to their parliaments; reduce the scope of the unanimity procedure; simplify and extend the co-decision between European Parliament and Council; streamline the Commission; make the Union more citizen-friendly and guarantee the citizens' fundamental rights. This, along with a decision to opt into economic and monetary union, would enable Britain to take its place at the heart of Europe, to the great and lasting benefit of the British people.

Building the Union: reform of the institutions [1]

The Intergovernmental Conference to be convened in 1996 will consider how to improve the European Union's institutions. The aim must be to ensure that the Union works to the fullest extent for the benefit of its citizens. The Community, now subsumed in the Union, has performed a remarkable service for Europeans. Its institutions have enabled it to do so. But they still have defects that must be remedied if they are to be both strong enough to face the challenges ahead, including the enlargement to Central and Eastern Europe, and open and democratic enough to earn the citizens' wholehearted support. This Paper suggests ways to remedy the defects.

The value of the Union and of its institutions

The period from 1914 to 1945 was dominated by the two World Wars, with the protectionist 1930s inbetween. Since then, Western Europe has enjoyed a time of unprecedented prosperity and peace. The European Community, and now the Union, has made a major contribution to this. From the customs union launched in the 1950s through to the single market programme completed in 1992, it has secured a large open market as a framework for prosperity. Its institutions and policies have provided a firm context for the Franco-German reconciliation and now for the safe anchorage of Germany, together with the other member states, in a Europe where instability to the East could only too easily spread westwards.

These achievements are due to the Community's capacity to deal with a fundamental problem for politics today: the continuing growth of interdependence, particularly among European countries. The member states can no longer conduct effective independent policies in fields where interdependence is far advanced: trade, where a firm mutual commitment is required to maintain an open market; currency, where the alternative to integration is not independence but domination by the strongest; the environment, where cross-border pollution requires common measures of control; and security, where the member states have been almost entirely reliant on American protection, but where Europeans now have to shoulder more of the responsibility themselves.

Europeans, including the British, need to work together intensively in these fields. The institutional question is how. There are two contrasting views of this, with a spectrum in between. One relies on intergovernmental cooperation, using as far as possible traditional diplomatic methods. The other regards the institutions developed by the Community as more effective for many purposes and having greater democratic potential, and seeks to enhance the effectiveness and democracy. This Paper takes the latter view. What this could mean in detail is considered later. Here we summarise what we see as the strengths and weaknesses of the institutions.

The Court of Justice has successfully ensured the rule of law within the Community for matters of Community competence, without which the single market, to take one example, would have no real substance. The principal problem that we shall consider here is the Court's lack of jurisdiction in, ironically, the Cooperation in Justice and Home Affairs.

The Council, where the member states are represented by their ministers, has been the Community's principal legislator and has taken substantial executive responsibility. The procedure of voting by qualified majority applies to most of the Community's legislation and the single market programme has shown it to be much more efficient than the unanimity procedure that prevailed before. British reactions to majority voting are often defensive. But many British interests in the Community could not be secured without it. The single market is one example; reform of the Common Agricultural Policy and conclusion of the Uruguay Round are others.

With majority voting you lose some as well as gain some. But it is a positive sum game, because it helps to deal effectively with problems that result from interdependence, which the member states can no longer resolve on their own. Formal sovereignty of member states or parliaments does not benefit the citizens where there is no real autonomy. This is a painful lesson for those who hold positions of national power to learn. But it will be more painful to ignore it. In the other two 'pillars' that the Maastricht Treaty set up alongside the Community, that is the Common Foreign and Security Policy and the Cooperation in Justice and Home Affairs, unanimity remains the rule. The question is whether that can be sustained, particularly as the number of member states increases.

2

Capping the Council is the European Council containing the heads of member states' governments. The Maastricht Treaty charged the European Council with giving the Union 'the necessary impetus for its development' and defining its 'general political guidelines' (Article D), and it continues to develop these roles.

Although a principal function of the Council is to enact Community laws, its method of work is more like that of a diplomatic conference than of a normal legislature. Of course the member states have to be represented in the system. But the way the Council has worked raises problems for democracies based on the principle of representative government. An answer to this problem has been found in the directly elected European Parliament, which has been given increasing powers by successive amending treaties and has on the whole played a constructive part, for example, again, in relation to the single market legislation. There will be proposals at the IGC to enhance the Parliament's powers.

The Community would not work without an effective executive or without an institution to articulate the common interest. It is not credible that the Council, or its network of committees bringing together officials from all the member states, could provide this. Thus the Commission performs a crucial function. Contrary to the picture painted by sections of the media and some politicians, the Commission is a rather small body, smaller than the average government department. Most of the execution of Community policy is carried out by the bureaucracies of the member states. But some policies, such as the competition policy, have to be undertaken independently of them; and there has to be a check as to whether what is agreed at Community level is in fact done. These are among the functions of the Commission. Hostility to the Commission, seen as an enemy of Britain, is misguided. The Commission has in fact been among Britain's best allies for reform of the CAP, liberal trade including the Gatt rounds, the single market, the control of state aids, and, when it was the major problem for British policy in the Community, Britain's contribution to the budget. Spleen vented against the Commission too often reflects frustration against the facts of interdependence, with which the Commission has been helping us to deal. But while the balance is positive, the Commission has its defects, some of which the IGC could help to remove.

Thus the institutions have made an essential contribution to the citizens' well-being. But they still have serious shortcomings. Reforms are needed to make them more open, democratic and effective.

The IGC and institutional reform

The IGC should work to improve the Union's institutions, not to broaden the range of its competences. The Maastricht Treaty requires it to examine certain institutional questions, including a reappraisal of the three-pillar structure of the Union, the widening of the scope of the co-decision procedure, and the classification of Community legislative acts in order to establish an 'appropriate hierarchy' among them. The European Council in June 1994 enlarged the terms of reference, setting up a 'Group of Reflection' which is, during the second half of 1995, to prepare for the IGC by considering measures 'deemed necessary to facilitate the work of the institutions and guarantee their effective operation in the perspective of enlargement'. The background to the IGC was considered in the first Paper in this series, on the *State of the Union*.[2] This explained why the Union and its institutions need substantial reform. Institutional tinkering will not measure up to the challenges the Union has to confront.

Enlargement is an historic challenge. The entry of Central and East Europeans will make the Union's member states more numerous and more diverse. Strong institutions will be required to avoid the risk of disintegration. The Union cannot be successfully enlarged without them. The single currency, which is more than likely to be introduced for at least a core of states by the end of the century, will also have significant institutional implications.[3] The reduction of the American contribution to Europe's defence will do the same. With the instability to the East, a stronger anchorage for the larger, united Germany has become yet more important. Among the causes of the disquiet of so many citizens following Maastricht, dissatisfaction with the form of democracy represented by the Union has been among the most significant. All these things make it urgent that the institutions of the Union be made more effective, democratic and citizen-friendly.

A short list of the proposals that we put forward to this end is given in the summary above and a full list in Annex One. The principal aims are to open up the Council to press and public and improve the accountability of the ministers to their parliaments; to make decision-taking more efficient by reducing the scope of the unanimity procedure; to simplify and extend the co-decision between European Parliament and Council; to streamline the Commission; and to guarantee the citizens' fundamental rights.

Without substantial results along such lines, there will be the danger for Europe that the Union will be progressively weakened, and for Britain that a core group of states, led by France and Germany, will seek to remedy this by proceeding with deeper integration without waiting for the more reluctant member states. Britain needs to avoid such an outcome, in order not to repeat the previous experience of failure to be in at the start and joining later on less favourable terms. A strong and democratic European Union is in the interests of Britain as much as of any other member state. Rather than opting out, Britain should seek to find ways in which states that are indeed unable to participate from the start can have derogations until such time as they can fully participate in the core, which should be progressively enlarged so as to include all member states of the Union. The IGC offers a chance to move ahead on such lines.

Making the Union work for the citizens

The Maastricht Treaty provides that all nationals of the member states are citizens of the Union with consequent rights and duties (Article 8 EC). No duties are listed and only a few rights, concerning free movement, local and European elections, consular protection, seeking the help of the Ombudsman, and petitioning the European Parliament. Many other rights are scattered throughout the Treaty, relating for example to freedom to pursue economic activity in any member state and equality between men and women. But there has been no attempt to list them prominently in the Treaty so that citizens can readily know what they are.

The Treaty does not, indeed, give any impression that citizens are central to the Union. Yet the Union will not provide the benefits of

5

which it is capable, perhaps not even survive, without the citizens' wholehearted support; and that will not be forthcoming unless the Union is working for them, responding to them and seen to be doing so. The Union needs to make its institutions more responsive to the citizens, and the Treaty should make their rights, and how they are to be guaranteed, crystal clear.

Article F of the Maastricht Treaty goes some way to define the rights that the Union's institutions are to respect, by reference to the European Convention on Human Rights and Fundamental Freedoms and to 'the constitutional traditions common to the Member States'. But that article is then excluded by Article L from the jurisdiction of the Court of Justice. The Treaty should assure citizens that they have this means of redress against actions of the Union. The guarantee should also be strengthened, as it is in all member states, by the Community acceding to the European Convention.[4]

The 'constitutional traditions common to the member states' include the right to elect representatives who enact laws and control the executive. While the Community has moved in that direction, it still falls quite far short. The governance of the Union is moreover complicated, obscure and little understood by the citizens. This has given rise to the drafting of constitutions intended to make the matter plain. These are not necessarily federal constitutions, as witness the proposal of the European Constitutional Group, which comes close to the British government's preferred solution of institutionalised Europe *à la carte*, with a weakening of the Commission, Parliament and Court.[5] The European Parliament's draft is of federal type, proposing co-decision, majority voting in the Council and responsibility of the Commission to the Parliament, together with citizenship based on the Union's own Bill of Rights.[6] It is vital that the Union should have a constitutional document that makes clear to the citizens what the Union's powers are and how its governance works. Such a document needs to be very thoroughly prepared. The IGC should provide for this process of preparation. Meanwhile the Community's legislative process, while very much better than no legislative process at all, needs to be simplified and made more efficient and easier for citizens to understand and to influence.

The legislative process

The Community is founded on law contained in the Treaties and in legislation enacted by the Community institutions. The benefits of the rule of law that this makes possible include not only the strength of the single market but also the fact that cross-frontier disputes are now resolved in the courts rather than through relationships based on relative power. But many people remain unaware of the benefits: partly because it is hard to get used to the multinational application of a principle that was formerly so predominantly national; partly because too much of the law-making process is obscure and remote from the citizens.

Obscurity and remoteness are not the only problems. Efficiency matters too. The legislative process devised for the Treaty of Rome was logical, with the Commission identifying the common European interest and the Council ensuring that the law proposed by the Commission corresponded with the ministers' views of their national interests. The Treaty provided for the phased introduction of qualified majority voting on most subjects, to avoid the paralysis that could result from a perpetual search for unanimity and the weakness of decisions based on the lowest common denominator. President de Gaulle's insistence on retaining the veto inhibited effective decisions in the Council for two decades, preventing among other things the passage of the legislation required to complete the single market. When qualified majority voting became normal for such legislation, following agreement on the Single European Act, the vast legislative programme required was carried through in not much more than five years. Even if ministers continued to seek consensus, this was more readily reached under what has been called 'the shadow of the vote', with compromise spurred by the fear of being voted down; and when necessary to reach a decision, votes were indeed taken. Even if each member state had its grievances about particular laws, all were content that the programme as a whole had been enacted. Thus the value of majority voting was demonstrated in practice; and the Council itself has confirmed the efficacy of the procedure.[7] It should be applied more widely, to make the Union more generally effective, especially as the further enlargement of the Union will make unanimity yet harder to attain.

The Council

The procedure of qualified majority already applies to most fields of Community legislation, though not to most of the decisions to be taken in the Union's other two pillars. Decisions that have the more constitutional implications, such as treaty amendment, accession of new member states and the ceiling of 'own resources', i.e. of tax revenue allocated to the Community, are still subject to unanimity and we do not propose that the IGC seek to change this. The European Parliament, in its report on the IGC, has taken the same view.[8] Unanimity will however be found increasingly impracticable in the future as the number of member states continues to increase, so that a very high qualified majority may have to be devised for at least some of these decisions. But there is already inadequate justification for requiring unanimity for decisions on Community matters such as the environment, development cooperation and the framework programmes for research and technological development. They should be transferred to qualified majority voting before the number of member states is further increased.

One question that will certainly arise at the IGC is the reform of the Council's voting system. The balance between larger and smaller states in the Union has already been disturbed by the recent enlargement; and since most of the candidates to come are small, each successive enlargement will, unless there is reform, increase the risk that states containing a large majority of the population of the Union will be outvoted in the Council by coalitions of smaller states. But changes in the weighting of votes require Treaty amendment; and the smaller member states are not likely to agree to a reduction of the weight given to their votes — at least unless it is linked to other changes that improve their relative position, such as reduction from two to one in the number of Commissioners to come from each of the larger member states. One reform of the voting system would be to leave the weighting of the smaller states as it is and increase that of the larger ones. Another would require that each decision be accepted by a 'double majority': both a weighted qualified majority, with more weight than at present for the larger states, and a qualified majority of the states with one vote each. Such a procedure is already provided for the Common Foreign and Security Policy (Article J.3.2) and the Cooperation in

Justice and Home Affairs (Article K.4.3). Our recommendation is for a simple version of double majority: a two-thirds majority with present weighting, provided that the states forming the majority contain at least two-thirds of the Union's population.

Another aspect of the Council that will be on the agenda in 1996 is its Presidency, occupied at present by each member state in turn for six months at a time. This turn as President helps to integrate each member state in the Community and Union system. But there are serious defects: the very long time, already over seven years, before a member state's turn comes round again; the interruption of business due to changes in priorities as between Presidencies; and the variable capacity to deal with problems of foreign and security policy in particular.

These defects have led to suggestions that the future system be based on the 'troika', which has been used to improve continuity in foreign policy cooperation and in the single market programme by bringing together the current, preceding and succeeding Presidencies. Such a group of states could remain in office for longer periods of say a year. Some proposals would arrange the troikas, at present based essentially on the alphabetical order for the succession of Presidencies, so that each would include one of the larger states. Others foresee groups of four rather than three. Yet others would compose regional groups of states. There is also a French proposal that the Council elect its President for a period of up to three years. Here we stay with the troika, which usually in any event includes one of the larger states.

The division of labour between the members of the troika could be adapted to the differing requirements of the Community and the CFSP. For Community matters, the Presidency of the Council is eased by the role of the Commission in maintaining coherence and initiative in the Community's programme and in conducting its external negotiations. The chairing of the different functional Councils — agriculture, transport, economic and financial, and so on — could be shared out among the different members of the troika. For the foreign and security policy, however, the Commission's role is weaker and the capacity of the larger member states is relatively more significant. So there would be merit in arranging the troikas so that each contains one of them, which in this field would be *primus inter pares*.

An additional way to make the Council more coherent would be to strengthen the element of continuity in the member states' delegations to it. The governments are represented in each Council by the ministers responsible for the subject with which that Council deals: ministers of agriculture in the Agriculture Council, ministers of transport in the Transport Council and so on. The element of continuity in the delegations that these ministers lead is provided at official level. There have been proposals that each state should be represented in all Councils by a Cabinet Minister for Europe. But that is hard to envisage because it would so radically change the balance of power within governments. More feasible is the idea that a Minister for Europe with the rank of Minister of State should participate in each state's delegations to all the Councils, facilitating coordination at the political level and providing an additional link between the Council and the member states' parliaments.

Democracy and parliamentary control

Community legislation has been enacted by the Council without press or public access to its sessions and without a published record of the proceedings. While there has recently been a certain opening up of some legislative sessions, public knowledge of the proceedings is still mainly derived, not from a proper official record, but from the often highly coloured and conflicting accounts given by individual ministers at their press conferences afterwards. Since the process takes the form of an intergovernmental negotiation, the diplomatic method of work is understandable. But the principle of representative government, that laws should be enacted by representatives of the citizens, answerable for their performance at elections, should not be forgotten. While the Council has produced considerable results, for example with the single market programme, its way of conducting business does not match up to proper standards of democratic accountability.

Michael Heseltine has explained that ministers are 'too busy to spend more than 5 to 10% of their time on the Council's affairs .... They fly in, read out their speech, listen wearily to eleven other speeches, then frequently find that it is too late to come to a conclusion, and take the next plane home'. So, he writes, much of the power lies with 'a myriad of bodies staffed by the civil servants' of the member states'. Without the work of their civil servants, ministers would indeed be unable to cope with their responsibilities in the Council. That is inevitable, given the nature of this curious legislative body. But the weakness of the means of accountability of the ministers for their performance is a major problem. It is not surprising if citizens are uneasy. One reform that we propose is to require that the Council's legislative sessions be open to the press and public and a full official record be published together with relevant documents. Those who know the Council well predict that decisive discussion will, if the formal proceedings are public, take place elsewhere – as they do indeed in national politics.[9] But public formal sessions, at which ministers should present their grounds for supporting or opposing the law in question, would nevertheless provide a sounder basis for their accountability, and would be seen by the citizens to do so. There is likewise a need for greater parliamentary control over the process, with respect to the roles of both the European Parliament and the member states' parliaments.

The member states' parliaments

If Community legislation had to be approved by fifteen, and eventually perhaps twice as many, member states' parliaments, there would be no Community legislation. As Heseltine put it, reacting to the idea that the UK Parliament might itself exercise control over the institutions of the Community, it is 'unrealistic to believe that it could ever have effective control or that other national parliaments, singly or acting together, could create an effective control mechanism'.[10] Common legislation is needed, and it has to be enacted by common institutions.

The idea that one such institution could be a Chamber of Parliamentarians or Committee of Parliaments, bringing together representatives of the member states' parliaments and sitting alongside the Council and the European Parliament, has come from sources such as Edouard Balladur and the European Policy Forum. We would reject such a reversion to a parliamentary body of a type that the Community had before 1979. The Community's legislative process is already complicated enough, without complicating it further with a third chamber that would necessarily be less effective than the European Parliament because its members, like the ministers in the Council but without the support they get from their officials, would be part-timers whose mandate would be different and whose main attention would be engaged elsewhere. The members of national parliaments would be better occupied ensuring proper accountability of their own ministers in the Council and working with members of the European Parliament to feed their concerns into its legislative work.

A Conference of Parliamentarians, or assises, was held in November 1990, bringing together representatives of the European Parliament and the member states' parliaments to discuss proposals for the IGC that resulted in the Maastricht Treaty. Declaration No. 14 attached to the Treaty favoured the holding of further such conferences, which could well be done in anticipation of the next IGC. Declaration No. 13 called for more exchange of information and contacts, especially 'reciprocal facilities and meetings between Members of Parliament interested in the same issues'. John Major said in a speech at Leiden University in September 1994, 'I see a case for Joint Committees (both by inviting MEPs to contribute to the national scrutiny committees, and vice versa) and we will examine this in the months ahead'.[11] The European Parliament and the member states' parliaments need each other's help. Because much of the Union's policy is executed by the member states, the European Parliament cannot properly scrutinise the execution without the cooperation of their parliaments. The checking of fraud connected with the Common Agricultural Policy is a clear example. Joint standing committees of MPs from member states' parliaments and MEPs could be particularly useful in such matters, as well as in following the progress of the Common Foreign and Security Policy and the Cooperation in Justice and Home Affairs. Ministers, Commissioners and the management of bodies such as Europol could be required to appear before them and reports would be made to both the European and the member states' parliaments. Such committees should be set up now, without waiting for the IGC, when their working could be reviewed in the light of experience.[12]

The member states' parliaments for their part need the sort of expertise that their compatriot MEPs possess, if they are to be effective in ensuring accountability of their ministers in the Council. There are understandable fears that stronger accountability could degenerate into such close control over the Council by the member states' parliaments as to turn it *de facto* into a legislature of fifteen parliaments, and soon more than that. But a Council with inadequate accountability will in the long run be ineffective because people will not regard the laws it enacts as genuinely legitimate. There has to be a balance between the right of member states' representatives in the Council to use their own judgement and that of the parliaments from whom they derive their legitimacy to hold them accountable; and that balance can surely not be based on secrecy of the Council's legislative sessions and lack of knowledge among Members of Parliament.

We have suggested that a Minister of State participating in the delegations to all Council meetings could help to strengthen the links between the Council and the parliaments. It has also been proposed that delegations to the legislative sessions could include members of their parliaments, which could then receive from their own representatives first-hand accounts of the proceedings. Better armed with the information that enables them to exercise accountability, the member states' parliaments would benefit all the more from the expertise that close cooperation with the MEPs could furnish them.

We also propose that member states' parliaments have the same access to the Court of Justice as the Union's institutions over questions of *ultra vires*. This means that the House of Commons could require the Court to review the legality of a Community Act on the grounds that the institutions were not competent to act, had not observed essential procedures, had misused their powers or infringed the Treaty or Community law.

The European Parliament's legislative role

The legislative role that the founding Treaties of the Community gave the European Parliament (then called Assembly) was consultative. But the difficulty of making the Council accountable, and a desire to move closer to the principles of representative government, brought the member states to accept a gradual strengthening of the Parliament's role in the course of four amending Treaties. The first two, in 1970 and 1975, gave it budgetary powers, on the insistence of the Dutch Parliament in particular, which could not accept that the tax money which was to pass direct to the Community should escape parliamentary control. Since Community expenditure could hardly be controlled by the several parliaments of the member states, budgetary powers for the European Parliament were the only viable solution. Then in 1987, with the ratification of the Single European Act, the Parliament's legislative powers were increased, particularly in view of the vast legislative programme to complete the single market; and the Maastricht Treaty further enhanced the Parliament's powers.

The Parliament has moved far towards co-legislation with the Council with respect to the budget, so that what the jargon calls the two arms of the budgetary authority act much like the two chambers of a federal legislature. Member states have, however, exerted themselves to keep preponderant power over the agricultural budget in the Council, without, it must be said, covering themselves with glory in that field.

The cooperation procedure, devised in the Single Act mainly for single market legislation, allows the Parliament to propose amendments which, if accepted by the Commission, can be rejected by the Council only if it is unanimous; and the Parliament can move rejection which, again, the Council can override only by unanimity. The Commission often does support the Parliament, as a result of which over half of its amendments have been accepted by the Council. The Maastricht Treaty extended the cooperation procedure to most fields of Community legislation, though not to the agricultural policy, where the Council continues to be the exclusive legislature.

The Maastricht Treaty also introduced the procedure of co-decision, which requires that legislation be accepted by both the Council and the Parliament in fifteen fields of Community competence, including the single market and the free movement of labour. This procedure allows the Parliament to propose amendments in a second reading; and when the Council does not agree with the amendments, the Conciliation Committee has to be convened, in which representatives of Parliament and Council seek agreement on a final text. The Council is encouraged to cooperate by the prospect that the Parliament may finally reject the bill, which co-decision gives it the right to do definitively. Co-decision at present applies to about one-quarter of the volume of Community legislation.

The assent procedure, introduced by the Single Act and extended by Maastricht, also requires acceptance by both the Council and the Parliament, but gives the Parliament no right to propose amendments. The Single Act applied this procedure to Treaties of accession and association, and the Maastricht Treaty added a range of international agreements and some internal matters, including the free movement of citizens and the uniform electoral procedure.[13]

Thus the Parliament has a real share of law-making power as well as substantial influence. It has been the butt of criticism, particularly in the British press. John Major also said at Leiden that the European Parliament 'is not the answer to the democratic deficit, as the pitiably low turn-out in this year's (1994) elections so vividly illustrated'. The turn-out was 56%, compared with 38% for the Congressional elections in the US later in the same year. The British turn-out in the European elections, at 36%, while comparable to that American one, was certainly far too low. But the turn-out in the rest of the Union was some 60%. Major went on to observe that there was 'an unrepresentative and rather incoherent range of parties in the new European Parliament' following those elections. If it is not representative of the voters, that must be largely due to the wide swing from Conservative to Labour among British MEPs, caused by the winner-takes-all system in the large constituencies for the European elections: the number of Conservative MEPs fell from 60 in 1979 to 18 in 1994, while those of Labour rose from 17 to 62. In all other countries and in Northern Ireland, the representation is proportional.

The extremely wide swings in British representation have provoked the criticism that the Parliament is less representative than it should be. The Treaty requirement of a uniform electoral procedure was moreover intended to make the elections a fully European event in which citizens would vote on European issues. The British government's refusal so far to agree to a uniform procedure is widely seen by Britain's partners to reflect indifference at best as to whether the citizens will view the Parliament as a properly influential democratic institution. A proposal that would allow considerable diversity among the member states within a framework of common principles is outlined in Annex Two. While any system that could attract a European consensus would inevitably be proportional, the proposal would exclude national lists, at present applied in France and Spain, which produce perfect proportionality but divorce MEPs from responsibility to individual constituents and give too much power to the party machine. Lists proposed by each party at regional level, from which MEPs would be elected in proportion to their party's share in the region's vote, would probably be preferred by most member states. But it would also be possible for Great Britain to retain its single-member constituencies for the majority of British MEPs, while securing proportionality as in German national elections through supplementary national lists. The proposal also provides for a minority of MEPs to be elected on European lists, which could attract more leading European politicians into the Parliament and would help to develop European political parties. The IGC should agree that a common electoral procedure, preferably along such lines, is to be introduced in good time for the next elections in 1999.

As regards Major's charge that the range of parties is incoherent, it is true that the Italian party system is in a state of flux and the French one is less stable than in most countries. But 70% of the MEPs nevertheless belong to one of the three main party groups and most of the rest are aligned with one or other of them. The picture of an incoherent Parliament based on a pitiable turn-out is not a fair one. Criticisms can be more justly directed at the poor attendance of MEPs from some member states - not, it must be said, the British. While better in the new Parliament than in previous ones, with some 400 MEPs generally attending the plenary voting sessions, attendance is still too low. The Parliament must put its house in order in this respect.

Despite its deficiencies, the Parliament has on the whole used its powers quite well; and the *Financial Times* probably had it right in its judgement that MEPs will 'be as responsible as their powers permit'.[14] The Parliament needs to be strengthened, not undermined; and its role needs to be made more clear to the citizens, in part by simplifying the dozen arcane procedures that the Treaties prescribe for Community legislation.

Strengthening the European Parliament

The argument for strengthening the European Parliament rests firmly on the need to apply the principles of representative government to those matters that the facts of interdependence render the member states unable to govern effectively on their own. It is the task of the MEPs to represent the citizens, which on the whole they do quite effectively within the limits of their powers. The Council represents the member states. This is a necessary function in a system with the federal characteristics that the Community has. But it is not the same as representing the individual citizens, which the Council is not designed to do. Unless the principle of representative government is rejected, the onus of proof is surely on those who contest the need for the Parliament to have legislative power.

The fear of many British MPs that more power for Strasbourg means less for Westminster is misplaced. Their legislative power, in fields of Community competence, has already been given by Treaty to the Council. Their influence over British ministers in the Council would remain. The European Parliament could not overrule the Council, for under any system of co-legislation both would have to accept the laws. Thus British MPs would retain precisely the same scope they have now to resist European legislation they do not like. All that they would lose is the chance of influencing British ministers to join with others in ramming through legislation against the wishes of the European Parliament. At present the Council can ignore the European Parliament except where co-decision, as defined in Article 189b EC, or the assent procedure applies; and it can ignore the member states' parliaments save when the Treaty is to be amended or the ceiling on the Union's budgetary resources is to be raised.

John Major said in his speech at Leiden that 'for now, it would be premature to consider a further increase in the Parliament's powers'. But delay carries risks. Public disillusion with the Union presents serious dangers; and citizens' interest in the Union's institutions will not be encouraged by keeping the Parliament as a kind of half-way house. German political leaders are deeply concerned about it. Wolfgang Schäuble and Karl Lamers, respectively Chairman and Foreign Affairs Spokesman of the CDU/CSU Parliamentary Party in the Bundestag, stressed in their influential paper, *Reflections on European Policy*, the importance of making the European Parliament 'a genuine law-making body with the same rights as the Council'.[15] There can be no doubt that this represents the thinking of the German coalition government and of the principal opposition party. The President of the Bundesbank has also repeatedly affirmed that a single currency requires a context of strong and democratic Union institutions. The Constitutional Court, in its judgment on the case brought against the constitutionality of the Maastricht Treaty, said it was 'crucial ... that the development of the democratic foundations of the Union keeps pace with integration'; and went on to observe that 'increasingly as the European nations grow together, democratic legitimacy is conferred within the structure of the European Union by the European Parliament'.[16] This judgment can be understood to require the German government to seek further extension of the Parliament's powers at the IGC.[17]

The British government may hope that a French predilection for governmental institutions, represented by the Council and the European Council, rather than parliamentary ones, will help to resist German pressure over the European Parliament's powers. But the partnership with Germany and the need to sustain German commitment to economic and monetary union are important enough to move France to concede significant progress towards European parliamentary democracy. Almost all other member states appear committed to strengthening the Parliament, from newly-joined Scandinavians in the North to Mediterranean countries that joined the Community in the 1980s precisely in order to consolidate their new democracies. Tony Blair, too, has indicated his support for a substantial extension of co-decision.[18] The widespread concern to strengthen the powers of the Parliament is justified. It would be very sad if Britain, with the longest parliamentary tradition in Europe, were to be the chief stumbling block.

The enlargement to Central Europe will strain the institutions, so it is better that reforms such as the strengthening of the Parliament be undertaken in time for them to be digested first; and it is fairer to the newcomers that they should see in advance what it is they will be joining. The problems for the Council will be particularly tricky as it has to adjust to the growing number of participants in what will certainly remain largely an intergovernmental negotiation. Although it is advisable that the number of MEPs be limited to no more than say 650 regardless of the number of member states — and this could be specified by the IGC — the Parliament's functioning will be less affected than that of the Council by the greater number of member states, so that it will, if it has appropriate powers, be better able to take its share of the strain. There is, then, a strong case for moving to a system in which approval of laws by both the Council and the Parliament is the norm, together with a simplification of the legislative procedures that will make them more comprehensible to those who are not immersed in the process.

The simplest and most comprehensible reform would be to apply the procedure of co-decision established by the Maastricht Treaty, amended to take account of the experience gained meanwhile, to virtually all Community legislation. One simplification of the procedure would be to enact laws immediately if the Council accepts the amendments proposed by the Parliament after its first reading, instead of proceeding with a second reading as at present. Another would be for the Parliament, if it decides neither to adopt nor to amend the 'common position' that the Council proposes to it, to convene immediately the Conciliation Committee to find out whether an accommodation may be possible. A proposal for a simplified co-decision procedure along such lines is shown in Annex Three. The procedure could also be made more efficient by setting time limits for the stages in the procedure for which the Council is responsible, as has already been done for the Parliament.

For the budget, the present procedures, which are a variant of co-legislation, could remain, although it is desirable to remove the stipulation that agricultural spending be separately classified as 'expenditure necessarily resulting from the Treaty or from acts adopted in accordance therewith' (Article 203 EC) and hence treated more as a preserve of the Council. The Parliament's influence over agricultural spending has increased since the medium-term 'financial perspectives' were introduced in 1988, bringing with them a joint control to ensure that the ceilings for agricultural as well as other main categories of expenditure are respected. But it would be reassuring to have proper parliamentary control in this field stipulated in the Treaty too. The distinction between 'compulsory expenditure', which includes agriculture, and 'non-compulsory expenditure', which includes almost everything else, should be abolished. It would likewise be proper that the elected representatives in the Parliament should shoulder their share of the responsibility for the size and form of the revenue for the budget. This would not enable them to force the Council to raise the revenue ceilings, but would require them to share the task of justifying the level and form of taxation to the citizens they represent.

The other major procedure that should be retained is assent, which could be extended to apply both to the revenue ceiling and to Treaty amendments. Here again the Parliament, without being able to oblige the Council or the member states to accept changes they did not want, would be required to take its share of accountability to the citizens. The procedure of consultation would remain for the field of Common Foreign and Security Policy in particular. This, together with the Parliament's role with respect to the Cooperation in Justice and Home Affairs, is considered later.

Improving the Commission

More even than the European Parliament, the Commission has been the butt of British media and politics. This stems in good part from resentment that interdependence requires us to act together with other Europeans instead of on our own account. The Commission is the obvious target, often being blamed for what the Council has decided.

The Commission is often attacked because it is not elected, and therefore not democratically responsible. The implication seems to be that the Council should have responsibility as the Union's executive. But democratic control of the Council is, as Heseltine pointed out, almost impossible to envisage; and an executive without proper democratic control can surely not be acceptable. Nor would such a complete fusion of legislative and executive powers in one body be healthy. Nor, for that matter, is it conceivable that the Council could be an effective executive. Even where execution is largely delegated to the administrations of the member states, there has to be a body independent of those administrations to ensure that it is being properly carried out; and in fields such as competition policy, where the administration cannot be delegated, the Council and its committees of officials do not present a plausible alternative to the Commission. One of the weaknesses of the Community is, indeed, that the Council keeps too many executive functions to itself, particularly by means of control of implementing regulations. We shall return to this. But given the difficulties of execution by the Council, which will escalate as the number of member states expands, it is surprising that so many critics fail to consider ways of making the Commission more responsible.

There have been proposals that the Commission, or at least its President, be directly elected, as in the US presidential system. A parliamentary executive is, however, the normal pattern among the member states and the Union has been moving towards this form of representative government. The European Parliament's votes on Jacques Santer and on the new Commission have demonstrated the new powers accorded it by the Maastricht Treaty, even if the Commission, while appreciating the legitimacy thus conferred on it, has commented that the time the procedure took, at seven months, was too long.[19] The Treaty (Article 158 EC) provided that the governments consult the Parliament before nominating the President 'by common accord', then consult the nominee about the other members of the Commission, before presenting their nominations for the Commission as a whole to the Parliament for its approval, which the Parliament is entitled to withhold. Thus the Parliament can reject the Commission explicitly and, it appears to follow, the President implicitly, since if the governments persisted in nominating a President of whom the Parliament disapproved, it would surely then reject the Commission as a whole. But while Maastricht has thus taken the Commission quite far towards becoming a parliamentary executive, the need to reach a compromise in negotiating the Intergovernmental Conference caused this to be done in a way that is not very clear to the citizens and is, indeed, inherently ambiguous. It would be better to make the Parliament's right to approve the President explicit. Jacques Santer went further in his inaugural address to the Parliament in January 1995, suggesting that it might choose one among a list of candidates presented by the governments.

Along with the charge that it is unelected, the Commission is often accused of being inefficient. Although it has suffered from all the problems of managing a multinational executive, the Commission has played an indispensable part in making the Community effective. Despite this notable performance, however, reform of its management, organisation and rules of procedure is required. While this is mainly a matter for the Commission itself, the IGC should consider whether Treaty amendment could also help to improve its efficiency.

A subject that will certainly be considered is the number of Commissioners. There are at present twenty, two each from the larger member states and one each from the others. If these criteria are used after further enlargement, the Commission could become intolerably unwieldy. One proposal is to reduce the number of Commissioners so that each would have charge of a major portfolio. That could at present imply, say, a dozen Commissioners. But those states from which there is no national in the Commission could well feel alienated from the institutions. The fact is that smaller states are not likely to accept the loss of their right to a Commissioner. The Commissioners should, however, be limited to a maximum of one per member state. Since the number of Commissioners will nevertheless be quite large, there is much to be said for increasing the number of Vice-Presidents from the two stipulated by the Maastricht Treaty, so that the President, together with the Vice-Presidents who would each be responsible for a major portfolio, could comprise a form of inner cabinet.

Laws and their execution: delegated legislation and administration

A further cause of inefficiency in the execution of Community laws and policies is the complex and cumbersome system of delegated, or implementing, legislation. All legislatures need to provide for such delegation, because there is too much detail in the governance of a modern polity for the legislature to cope with it all; and the legislature should not try to become the executive. The question is how and where to draw the line.

In the UK the delegation takes the form of Statutory Instruments. Most of these have the force of law when issued but may be annulled on request of either House within forty days, not counting those on which Parliament is in recess. For some of the most significant Instruments, however, enactment has to await approval by Parliament. Each Instrument must be accepted or rejected as a whole; and a Joint Committee of both Houses reviews them all to ensure that correct procedures are followed.

The British system works fairly well. But the same cannot be said of the Community's. The Council and its committees of officials interfere too much in the Commission's executive function, prejudicing efficiency and deepening opacity. In place of the two procedures in Britain, the Council has no fewer than seven procedures for supervising the Commission's implementing decisions. There are the 'advisory committees', which provide the benefit of liaison with the officials of member states without hampering the Commission's execution of Community business. There are two procedures for 'management committees', whereby a qualified majority of the member states' officials can delay the application of the Commission's texts or refer them to the Council. Given the requirement of a qualified majority to prevent the Commission from acting, these committees have not interfered too much in the Commission's executive task. Then there are two more procedures for 'regulatory committees', which require only a blocking minority to delay or refer; and these can seriously impede the dispatch of business by the Commission. Finally there are two more procedures whereby any member state can refer a safeguard measure, taken to protect an industrial sector from uncomfortable imports, to the Council for a variety of further decisions.

These Byzantine arrangements cry out for simplification and reform. This was the intention of Article 10 of the Single Act and of Declaration 16 attached to the Maastricht Treaty presaging consideration by the next IGC of 'the classification of Community acts with a view to establishing an appropriate hierarchy between the different categories of act', so as to distinguish between more important and less important legislation and to clarify whose responsibility it is to do what. The British aim should surely be to improve the Community's efficiency by moving as fast as possible towards a system such as the one that works quite well in Westminster and Whitehall. Without such movement, the present system would deteriorate exponentially in line with future enlargements.

Once the implementing legislation has been passed, most of the consequent executive function is performed by the civil services in the member states. This enables the Commission to remain a rather small organisation, confined mainly to the drafting of legislation and the oversight of its execution, while itself being directly responsible for only a limited range of executive tasks. But while the principle of delegated administration is sound, it does depend on adequate supervision of the performance of member states' civil services. Those states that do not fulfil their obligations can undermine the effectiveness of the Union and gain unfair advantages over those that do. This is felt keenly by the British government, which pressed successfully for sanctions to be stipulated by the Maastricht Treaty in the form of fines that the Court of Justice can, on proposal of the Commission, impose on offending member states. The Court of Auditors has indicated, however, that all remains far from well, at least as regards fraud and lax financial control by member states in spending Community money; and the same may be surmised with respect to other aspects of member states' execution of their Community obligations.

The British government will surely wish to consider whether there are further ways in which the next IGC could agree to clean up this rather murky corner of the Community's affairs. One way would be to require that each government should stipulate how it will carry out its share of implementation of the laws enacted in the Council. Governments may choose different ways to fulfil their legal obligations, but their choice would be transparent, subject to peer review, and more readily monitored by parliaments, local governments, the Court of Auditors and the Commission. But the Commission should also act more effectively to ensure that proper implementation does in fact take place. It has until recently been much absorbed in the legislative programme to complete the single market. Now that is largely complete, the Commission should concentrate on ensuring that the laws are properly implemented. For this it needs adequate staff, for which the Union's budget should provide, and legal powers, which are a matter for the IGC. The IGC should act to strengthen the Commission's powers to ensure the implementation of the Community's laws and policies as well as to check fraud and lax financial control and to bring the perpetrators to book, where appropriate with criminal charges.

Proposals to establish 'an appropriate hierarchy' of Community acts likewise have the intention of confining the content of Community laws to the essentials, while leaving the details to the member states. Thus Community laws can comprise a minimal framework that defines the rights and duties of citizens and legal persons, provides for a level playing field and non-discrimination, stipulates strict control over the spending of Community money, and lays down any other essential principles and rules. This was the intention of the original definition, in the Rome Treaty, of a Community Directive: that it should be binding regarding the 'result to be achieved' but leave the member states to enact their own legislation as to the 'choice of form and methods' (Article 189 EC). One might expect that their representatives in the Council would ensure that member states retain the degree of autonomy offered by the Directive, and that their parliaments would seek to keep them up to the mark in this. But, although the single market programme, with its New Approach to Standards, developed a technique that applied the principle of subsidiarity, it seems that the potential of the Directive for doing so has not in general been adequately exploited. The IGC should seek ways to ensure that fuller use is made of it, while at the same time ensuring that the Commission has the resources required to check that the member states' legislation does in fact provide properly for the realisation of the 'result to be achieved'.

The Court of Justice and the rule of law

One of the greatest merits of the European Community has been the rule of law applied without discrimination direct to individuals, companies, member states and Community institutions. Community law has been administered, mainly by the courts of member states but with the European Court of Justice in Luxembourg at the apex of the system, within the whole range of Community competence: economic, environmental and to some extent social.

There are those who resent what they see as an 'activist' Court of Justice. Doubtless that institution is not perfect. But it has played an essential part in the success of the Community and in particular in the single market programme. It has earned a large measure of respect among the legal profession in Britain as well as other countries. The rule of law has replaced power relationships as the context within which the different member states and their citizens transact their business with each other. This is one of the reasons why the political relationships among them are so much better than before World War Two. It is dangerous to seek to undermine it. The question should not be how to chip away at this common legal system, but whether it can be strengthened, and if so how.

Reforms that could help to strengthen it will be considered in a forthcoming *Federal Trust Paper* on 'Justice and Fair Play'. One question that is raised by the growth in the number of member states concerns the number of judges in the Court. Up to now, there has been one for each member state, plus one more when there is an even number of states. But the Court has to sit, for some important cases, in plenary session (Article 165 EC); and it risks becoming unwieldy as the number of member states grows. Either the obligation to sit in plenary session should be removed or a system of rotation among the member states adopted. There can in any case be a national of each state in the Court of First Instance, which carries part of the workload. It may indeed be desirable to increase the number of Courts of First Instance, and hence of judges, as that workload increases, following the pattern of the Divisions of the High Court.

While the competences of the Court of Justice enable it to play an effective part in the Community, the same cannot be said of the Union's other two 'pillars'. For the Common Foreign and Security Policy, the Court has no competence, and while this is a field of policy rather than law, the Court should have jurisdiction at least where the rights of individuals are affected, and perhaps as regards the fulfilment of Treaty procedures and obligations as well. For the Cooperation in Justice and Home Affairs the Court is also excluded unless the governments specifically negotiate conventions that provide for its jurisdiction. Thus citizens can lack adequate legal remedies in fields where their rights may be heavily involved. There is no valid justification for excluding the Court from these fields.

Although the Maastricht Treaty affirms that the Union is to respect fundamental rights, here again the Court of Justice is not given jurisdiction. The Court has itself, in its case law, required that the institutions respect the rights guaranteed by the European Convention and by the 'constitutional traditions common to the Member States', as the Treaty puts it, on the grounds that its duty is to ensure that the Community law is observed and it can hardly expect the member states to observe it if fundamental rights are not respected. But citizens can be forgiven for not knowing that the Court has reasoned in this way. It would surely be better if the Treaty explicitly charged the Court with the task of ensuring that the institutions respect the rights.

Subsidiarity

Article A of the Maastricht Treaty affirms that 'decisions are taken as closely as possible to the people'. This is an aspiration rather than a fact, particularly in a state as centralised as the United Kingdom. But it is in Article 3b EC that the Treaty makes the principle operational, by requiring the Community to act only where the objectives 'cannot be sufficiently achieved by the Member States and can therefore, by reason of the scale or effects of the proposed action, be better achieved by the Community'. This points to another way of preventing the Council and the European Parliament from getting involved in too much detail: if the Community doesn't have to do it, leave it to the member states.

One way of preventing unnecessary interference by the Community is to entrust as much as possible of the execution of Community law and policy to the member states. This is done in the judiciary, where most cases that arise under Community law are tried in the courts of the member states. It is also, as we saw, largely true of administration.

More fundamentally, it is time to consider whether the Treaty could do more to define the limits of the Union's competence. The Union now has a wide enough range of competences to do what the logic of interdependence requires it to do in the economic field, and probably in those of social policy and the environment, although further competence in the fields of defence and in energy policy may one day be desirable. Yet there is widespread concern that the Union and the Community will spread into ever wider spheres of action; and this general worry inhibits objective consideration of the institutional reforms that are still so necessary. There is much to be said for drawing up a list of competences that, unless the member states agree to further Treaty amendment, would be specifically reserved to the member states. As in the Canadian constitution, in between this list and that of the exclusive competences already accorded to the Union would be the area of shared competence. But such a list would require very thorough preparation, by what would amount to a constitutional conference. So it is not a matter for the forthcoming IGC.

The Maastricht Treaty, although enunciating the principle that decisions be taken as closely as possible to the people, does not venture to apply that principle to the member states' internal affairs. But it does approach more closely to the people as far as Community affairs are concerned, by establishing the Committee of the Regions to advise on matters that concern regional or local government. This has the merit of bringing into the Community's policy-making system representatives closer to the citizens than are the governments' representatives in the Council. There has been pressure from within the Assembly of European Regions to limit membership of the Committee to representatives of regions, though this does not seem practicable in the absence of regional authorities in some member states. There have also been proposals to transform the Committee into a chamber with legislative powers. It is surely not desirable to complicate the legislative process yet further by adding a third chamber to the Council and the European Parliament. But the Committee should be treated as an important advisory body. It should be given its own budget and secretariat, instead of sharing a 'common organisational structure' with the Economic and Social Committee as a Protocol to the Maastricht Treaty stipulates.

Common Foreign and Security Policy

The institutional arrangements for both the Common Foreign and Security Policy (CFSP) and the Cooperation in Justice and Home Affairs (CJHA) are more intergovernmental than those of the Community. There is the exclusion of the Court of Justice, apart from those CJHA conventions that may provide for its jurisdiction (Article K.3.2.c of the European Union Treaty). The Commission's right of initiative to make proposals is not exclusive. The European Parliament is to be informed and consulted (Articles J.7, K.6) but has no powers. Thus the role of these three Community institutions is rather weak. How far is this justified by inherent differences between these fields and those for which the Community is responsible?

Defence is certainly very different from the Community's existing fields of competence, to a point where it has been suggested that France may propose a fourth pillar for defence alone. It is certainly to be recommended that those heads of governments of member states that are also members of the Western European Union should seek to strengthen defence cooperation in a separate session after each meeting of the European Council. Such matters will be considered in a subsequent *Federal Trust Paper* on the Common Foreign and Security Policy. Here we are concerned only with some aspects of the relationship of the CFSP to the Union's institutions.

First, it should be borne in mind that the Community already has a powerful external economic policy, for which the Commission acts as negotiator, the Council votes by qualified majority and the Parliament has the right of assent over many bilateral and international agreements. The results in the Gatt and the Lomé Convention demonstrate the effective impact of the Community in these fields. Although the Community's policies towards Central and Eastern Europe have been criticised as too protectionist, taken as a whole they have had an immensely beneficial effect on the Eastern neighbours, from 1989-90 with the initial liberalisation and grant of generalised preferences and of the Phare aid programme, through the Europe Agreements and up to the commitment to future accession. This contrasts sharply with the performance of the foreign policy cooperation, now under the banner of CFSP, with respect to Central and Eastern Europe, and notably former Yugoslavia. With the introduction of the single currency, further power will be added to what should surely be called the 'common foreign and economic policy'. The conclusion can hardly be escaped that, where the Community's institutional structure can be applied, it is more effective than a more intergovernmental system.

While defence is clearly different, requiring different types of decision and having different implications for sovereignty, there are areas of foreign policy that are not closely defence-related but are not at present within the competence of the Community. A number of such areas were, before Maastricht, covered by the European Political Cooperation. If we want the Union to be more effective in such fields, we should make more use of the Community's successful experience. The best solution would be to transfer them into Community competence, with the procedure of qualified majority voting applicable, at least after a transitional period. Consultation of the Parliament should also apply to common positions and joint actions, rather than just to the 'main aspects and basic choices', as Article J.7 of the Maastricht Treaty provides. Alternatively, such fields could be set aside for joint action using the qualified majority procedure, as provided in Article J.3. It must not be forgotten that unanimous decisions will become more and more difficult to achieve as the Union is enlarged; and the alternative of resorting to action by variable groups of member states would forgo the major potential of a Union that combines the strength of all the member states. But while majority voting should become a mainstream procedure in the fields that are not defence-related, it would be advisable to allow member states, at least during a transitional period, to opt out of joint actions that are particularly sensitive for them, for example, as far as Britain is concerned, possible actions relating to Commonwealth countries.

The Maastricht Treaty provided that the President of the Council shall represent the Union in CFSP matters. Denmark set an example to member states that do not belong to WEU by renouncing its right to the Presidency where decisions and actions of the European Union with defence implications are on the agenda, as well as representation of the European Union in international organisations, international conferences and with third countries.[20] The presence of three new member states with a tradition of neutrality has accentuated the problem of decision-taking in the Union with respect to defence-related foreign policy. The ways of dealing with this are likely to include confining the right to vote as well as to preside over the Council regarding such matters to the states that are prepared to make a full contribution to defence cooperation, and accepting that states may stand aside from actions in which they do not wish to participate.

It was suggested above that, if a troika system is introduced as a general way of dealing with the problem of the Presidency, the larger state in each group could have the leading role in CFSP matters. Defence would be the clearest case where this should apply. If fields not related to defence were transferred to Community competence, however, the Commission would become the normal negotiator, which would help to ease the problem of dividing responsibilities between larger and smaller states in the group.

Cooperation in Justice and Home Affairs

Although Cooperation in Justice and Home Affairs is also largely concerned with security, this time internal security, it differs sharply from the CFSP, not least because of its intense implications for fundamental rights. This makes the question of judicial remedies particularly sensitive. The inadequacy of current means of redress was noted earlier. While the international conventions that the Maastricht Treaty envisages may provide for the jurisdiction of the Court of Justice, they may also not do so. The CJHA procedures have moreover been slow to produce results, although there are some urgent matters requiring settlement, in fields such as asylum, immigration, drug trafficking and international fraud. There is growing concern that necessary decisions should be taken without delay and that the resulting rules should show proper respect for fundamental rights, with adequate remedies provided.

The fields of competence of the CJHA come close to those of the Community in many respects, in particular because both have responsibilities relating to free movement of people. This has been recognised in the case of visas, which are to be regulated as from 1 January 1996 by Community procedures, including qualified majority voting (Article 100.c.3 EC). Various proposals for reform will be considered in detail in the forthcoming *Federal Trust Paper* on the subject. Here we suggest only that the scope for qualified majority voting be widened in order to make decision-taking more efficient, and that the roles of the Court of Justice and the Parliament be enhanced in the interests of fair and open government in fields so sensitive for fundamental rights. The transfer of the CJHA pillar into Community competence would be the simplest and best solution.

Core group, variable geometry

The CDU/CSU paper by Schäuble and Lamers emphasised the vital importance for Germany both of enlarging the Union towards Central and Eastern Europe and of 'deepening' it so that it will still be strong enough to work effectively. Their aim is 'to strengthen the EU's capacity to act and to make its structures and procedures more democratic and federal'. It is sometimes said that when Germans use the word 'federal' they mean 'decentralised' whereas the British mean 'centralised'. For the division of competences between the member states and the centre, a federal system has to have elements of both: some powers, including, for example, trade and money, exercised by the centre; others, following the other aspect of subsidiarity, remaining with the states. But Schäuble and Lamers were at that point writing not about the competences but about the institutions, which in a federal system are those of constitutional democracy at each level: implying, for the Community, a two-house legislature comprising the European Parliament 'with the same rights as the Council', and with the Commission as the executive taking on 'features of a European government'. They went on to question the retention of the principle of unanimity for treaty amendment and to affirm that 'no country should be allowed to use its right of veto to block the efforts of other countries more able and willing to intensify their cooperation and deepen integration'. They had in mind a core group of countries that would press ahead with further integration, while remaining 'open to every member state willing and able to meet its requirements'.[21] Meanwhile, this 'variable geometry' or 'multi-speed' approach should as far as possible be 'institutionalised in the Union Treaty'. There is strong support among the German political establishment for the general drift of their views; and, without expressly endorsing them, Chancellor Kohl has indicated that the Union's development must not be held back to the pace of the most reluctant member.

In France, Alain Lamassoure, as Minister for European Affairs, put forward somewhat similar proposals for a 'new founding contract' among a core group of states that would adopt all measures of integration in full and organise themselves to work together and to prepare common positions in the Union.[22] Valéry

Giscard d'Estaing proposed a core group comprising France, Germany and Benelux.[23] Edouard Balladur has envisaged overlapping cores for subjects such as currency and defence, with the Franco-German partnership clearly at the centre of each. Jacques Chirac has expressed similar views.

The British government has preferred to stress the single market as the unifying element for all member states, with freedom for them to opt into or out of other policies and with future development based on intergovernmental rather than Community institutions. The institutional arrangements for such a Union *à la carte* would certainly deprive member states that opt out of policy fields of their right to vote and probably to participate in Council meetings on those subjects and could restrict the roles of their nationals in other institutions too. There are precedents in the Social Protocol and the economic and monetary union. Advocates of such a flexible union have contended that it would be easier for Central and East European states to join. But while at least some of them will need transitional periods before they can participate fully in all fields, they are not likely either to be accorded or to seek a permanent right to opt out such as Britain and Denmark have obtained; and member states with finite transitional periods have in the past been granted full voting rights.

The prospect is, then, that with limited exceptions among existing member states, the element of variable geometry will be temporary, taking the form of different speeds towards full participation in all fields rather than permanently different tiers. But France, Germany and a number of other member states, together with the Commission and the European Parliament, will fear that the Union would meanwhile be seriously weakened. They are not likely to deflected from moving in the direction of a core, whether based on perhaps half a dozen member states that will be the first to adopt the single currency, or on those that accept the full range of integrated activities including currency and defence, or on a strengthened partnership between France and Germany, based on a revised Franco-German Treaty, to guide the development of overlapping cores. In either case, core members would, as Lamassoure suggested, 'organise themselves to work together'; and they could well proceed to set up some institutions of their own alongside the Union.

If Britain cannot bring itself to accept the full range of integration, it would be better to cooperate in finding a way for core states to deepen their integration within, as far as possible, the Union's institutions, in order to limit the distance between the core and the rest and to facilitate a subsequent rapprochement. This might take the form of amending Article N of the Maastricht Treaty, which at present requires unanimity for any treaty amendment, so as to provide that amendments allowing a group of member states to proceed to deepen integration within the Union could be adopted by a qualified majority of member states.

But any formal arrangement for a core group is only a second best. It is much better that all member states be committed to the whole range of integration. If there has to be a core, moreover, there is no satisfactory role for Britain marginalised outside it. If a core is formed, it will tend to develop its own momentum. Britain lost enough through failure to join the original Community core in the 1950s. We should not repeat that mistake in the 1990s.

Towards a democratic and effective Union: priorities for the IGC

All the Union's institutions need to be made stronger. The Council needs a qualified majority procedure that protects the interests of both large and small states; it needs to reform the Presidency system; and it needs to relinquish the veto except for matters with constitutional implications and for defence-related decisions. Without such reforms, it will be unable to take the strain of future enlargement. The Parliament should have a general right of co-decision with the Council. The Commission should have a clear accountability to the Parliament and greater powers to ensure the proper implementation of Community acts by member states. The Court should have explicit jurisdiction in the field of fundamental rights and the Community should accede to the European Convention. The institutional arrangements for the CJHA should be brought into line with those of the Community, preferably by a transfer of competence to the Community in this field; and the same applies to the areas of the CFSP that are not defence-related, while defence remains in a separate pillar.

Germany is particularly concerned about co-decision for the Parliament, and about moving towards the application of Community procedures to the CJHA and towards majority voting for the non-defence-related CFSP. France is not enthusiastic about these institutional reforms but is insistent on moving to stage three of economic and monetary union without too much delay. In return for German cooperation in this, France is likely to go far enough to satisfy Germany as regards institutional reform. The essential minimum for Britain to accept in order to enable the Union to proceed confidently towards further enlargement is, then, a sufficient measure of the institutional reform. This, together with opting into the economic and monetary union, would also go far to exclude the risk of a core being established without Britain.

Thus a constructive British approach to reform of the Union's institutions is needed, aiming in particular to open up the Council and improve the accountability of ministers to their parliaments; to reduce the scope of the unanimity procedure; to simplify and extend the co-decision between the European Parliament and the Council; to streamline the Commission; and to make the Union more citizen-friendly and guarantee the citizens' fundamental rights. An effective policy such as this would, with the decision to opt into economic and monetary union, enable Britain to take its place at the heart of a successful European Union, to the great and lasting benefit of the British people.

NOTES

[1] The main contributor to this Paper was John Pinder. He was assisted by a working party composed of members of the Round Table under the chairmanship of David Martin MEP.

[2] Federal Trust Papers Number One, *State of the Union*, London, Federal Trust, February 1995.

[3] Federal Trust Papers Number Two, *Towards the Single Currency*, London, Federal Trust, May 1995.

[4] This has been proposed by, among others, the European Parliament; see A.G. Toth, *The Oxford Encyclopaedia of European Community law: Vol.1, Institutional Law*, Oxford University Press, 1990, p.291.

[5] *A Proposal for a European Constitution*, Report by the European Constitutional Group, London, 1993.

[6] *Second Report of the Institutional Committee on the Constitution of the European Union*, rapporteur Fernand Herman, European Parliament, A3-0064/94, 9 February 1994. For the draft Bill of Rights, see 'Declaration of Fundamental Rights and Freedoms', the European Parliament, 12 April 1989, *Official Journal*, 1989, C120/51.

[7] J.H.H. Weiler, 'The Transformation of Europe', *The Yale Law Journal*, Vol.100, No.8, June 1991, p.2461.

[8] 'The Council Report on the Functioning of Maastricht', *Agence Europe*, 23 March 1995.

[9] 'Plenary Session of the European Parliament', *Agence Europe*, 18 May 1995.

[10] Michael Heseltine, *The Challenge of Europe; Can Britain Win?*, London, Weidenfeld and Nicolson, 1989, pp.25, 31.

[11] See for example William Nicoll, 'Representing the States', in Andrew Duff, John Pinder and Roy Pryce (eds), *Maastricht and Beyond: Building the European Union*, London, Routledge for the Federal Trust, 1994, p.192.

[12] Op. cit., pp.25-6.

[13] The Rt Hon John Major MP, 'Europe: A Future that Works', William and Mary Lecture given at the University, Leiden, 7 September 1994.

[14] This approach seems now to be favoured by the European Parliament: see its *Resolution on the functioning of the Treaty on European Union with a view to the 1996 IGC: Implementation and Development of the Union*, A4-0102/95, 17 May 1995.

[15] See Richard Corbett, 'Representing the People', in Duff, Pinder and Pryce (eds), op. cit., p.226.

[16] Ibid., pp.225-6.

[17] Op. cit.

[18] Leading article, *Financial Times*, 16 January 1995.

[19] Op. cit.

[20] Wolfgang Schäuble and Karl Lamers, *Reflections on European Policy*, CDU/CSU Fraktion des Deutschen Bundestages, Bonn, 1 September 1994, translated and reprinted in Lamers, *A German Agenda for the European Union*, London, Federal Trust and Konrad Adenauer Stiftung, 1994, citation from p.15.

[21] Federal Constitutional Court, *Judgment delivered on 12 October 1993 on the Constitutional Appeal against the Treaty of Maastricht*, C.I.b2.

[22] Professor Dr Ulrich Everling, *The Maastricht Judgment of the Federal Constitutional Court and its Significance for the Development of the European Union*, Occasional Paper 2, Europa Institute, University of Edinburgh, May 1995.

[23] The Rt Hon Tony Blair MP, 'Britain in Europe', address given at the Royal Institute of International Affairs, 5 April 1995.

[24] European Commission, *Rapport sur le fonctionnement du Traité sur l'Union Européenne*, SEC(95) 731 final, Brussels, 10 May 1995, para. 25.

[25] See Alastair Sutton, 'European Union and the Rule of Law, Part II: Justice and Fair Play in the European Union', in Duff, Pinder and Pryce (eds), op. cit, p.264.

[26] Op. cit., pp.284-7.

[27] European Council in Edinburgh, 11-12 December 1992, *Conclusions of the Presidency*, Part B, Annex 1, Section C.

[28] Op. cit., p.15.

[29] Ibid., pp.16-17.

[30] *Le Monde*, 30 May 1994.

[31] *Le Figaro*, 10, 11 January 1995.

ANNEX ONE

List of Proposals

This Annex lists the proposals recommended or suggested in the text. Most require Treaty amendments. Some could be dealt with by Declarations attached to an amending Treaty. All should be part of the complex of institutional questions to be considered at the IGC.

1. The Court of Justice should have jurisdiction regarding the respect by the Union of fundamental rights.

2. The Community should accede to the European Convention for the Protection of Human Rights and Fundamental Freedoms.

3. The IGC should lay down a process for converting the Treaty into a constitutional document that makes clear to the citizens what the Union's powers are and how its governance works.

4. The qualified majority voting procedure should apply to Community decisions on the environment, development cooperation and research and technological development, with unanimity retained for decisions with the more constitutional implications, such as treaty amendment, accession of new states and the ceiling of 'own resources'.

5. The qualified majority procedure should be amended to require a two-thirds majority with present weighting provided that the majority includes states containing at least two-thirds of the Union's population.

6. The Presidency of the Council should comprise the representatives of a group of three member states, each such troika to serve for one year. For EC affairs, the members of the troika would share out among themselves the chairing of the different functional Councils. For Common Foreign and Security Policy the representative of the largest of the three states could be *primus inter pares.*

7. Member states should include in their delegations to all Council meetings, in addition to the specific departmental ministers, Europe Ministers with the rank of Ministers of State, to provide an element of continuity at the political level, as well as an additional channel of accountability to the member states' parliaments.

8. The Council's legislative sessions should be open to press and public and a full official record should be published.

9. Joint committees of MPs and MEPs should be set up to deal with such matters as fraud where responsibilities are shared between the Union and the member states.

10. Member states' delegations to the Council's legislative sessions should include representatives of the ministers' parliaments, whose reporting to the parliaments would provide a further opportunity to ensure accountability.

11. Member states' parliaments should be able to require the Court of Justice to review Community acts on grounds of *ultra vires*.

12. A common procedure for elections to the European Parliament should be introduced in good time for the 1999 elections. (See Annex Two)

13. Laws should be approved by both Council and European Parliament and the present co-decision procedure should be simplified. (See Annex Three)

14. The distinction between 'compulsory' and 'non-compulsory' expenditure should be abolished, thus bringing the agricultural budget under the control of the Parliament as well as the Council. The Parliament's assent should be required for raising the ceiling of revenue for the Union's budget as well as for Treaty amendment.

15. The European Parliament should have the power to approve the President of the Commission.

16. The number of Commissioners should be reduced to a maximum of one from each member states. Six Vice-Presidents could be selected from among the Commissioners to comprise a form of inner cabinet.

17. The procedure for implementing legislation should be simplified by making it more like that of British Statutory Instruments.

18. Each government should be required to stipulate how it will carry out its share of the implementation of Community laws and policies. The Commission should have stronger powers to investigate suspected failure of implementation, to check lax financial control by member states in spending Community money, and, where fraud is detected, to bring criminal charges.

19. In order to limit the number of judges trying cases in the Court of Justice, either the number of judges should be kept below the number of member states as that is enlarged, or the Court should no longer be obliged to sit for certain cases in plenary session.

20. The Court of Justice should have jurisdiction with respect to the Cooperation in Justice and Home Affairs and, at least where the rights of individuals are concerned, to the Common Foreign and Security Policy.

21. The IGC should apply the principle of subsidiarity to Community legislation, by seeking ways to ensure that fuller use is made of Directives, which are binding regarding 'the result to be achieved' but leave the member states to choose 'the form and methods'.

22. The Committee of the Regions should be given its own budget and secretariat..

23. Those heads of governments of member states that are also members of WEU should seek to strengthen defence cooperation by meeting in a separate session after each meeting of the European Council.

24. The qualified majority procedure should be increasingly applied to those areas of the Common Foreign and Security Policy that are not defence-related.

25. The roles of the Court of Justice and the European Parliament in relation to the Cooperation in Justice and Home Affairs should be enhanced and the scope for qualified majority voting widened, preferably by transferring that pillar into Community competence.

26. In order to prevent a weakening of the Union as it enlarges, with a growing number of derogations as well as existing opt-outs from particular policies, France and Germany may well lead other states that apply the full range of integration, to form a core group of states organising a closer cooperation among themselves. A way should be found for core states to deepen their integration within, as far as possible, the Union's institutions. This might take the form of amending Article N of the Maastricht Treaty so that amendments allowing a group to deepen integration within the Union could be adopted by a qualified majority of member states.

27. If any such core is formed, Britain should be part of it.

28. In order that Britain together with the other member states can move confidently towards the enlargement, we recommend a positive British approach to the reform of the institutions, with priority for those proposals listed above that would:

- open up the Council to public scrutiny and improve the accountability of the ministers to their parliaments;
- reduce the scope of the unanimity procedure;
- simplify and extend the co-decision between European Parliament and Council;
- streamline the Commission;
- make the Union more citizen-friendly and guarantee the citizens' fundamental rights.

ANNEX TWO

DRAFT PROPOSAL FOR THE UNIFORM ELECTORAL PROCEDURE OF THE EUROPEAN PARLIAMENT [1]

The European Parliament,

Having regard to Article 138 (3) of the Treaty on European Union, which obliges the Parliament to draw up proposals for elections by direct universal suffrage in accordance with a uniform electoral procedure in all Member States;

Noting that the Parliament has now been elected four times by different electoral procedures in all Member States;

Requests the Council, acting unanimously, to lay down provisions and recommend them for adoption in accordance with the respective constitutional requirements of each Member State, on the following basis:

1.   Members of the European Parliament should be elected according to the principle of proportional representation;

2.   60% of the seats shall be distributed on the basis of regional constituencies; 25% on the basis of the national territory of Member States; and 15% on the basis of the European Union as a whole;

3.   Member States may seek derogations from this scheme of distribution to take account of special regional features;

4.   According to the principle of subsidiarity, a Member State may choose the electoral procedures for the regional and national elections within its own territory as long as the overall result in that State ensures that the distribution of seats corresponds to the proportion of the total votes cast;

5.   Election from the European Union lists shall be by panachage with each elector having a maximum of four votes; [2]

Urges the Council to present to the Parliament the appropriate draft provisions within a period of three months, and insists that, if necessary after conciliation, and once having received the assent of the Parliament by absolute majority of its Members, the Council and Member States act decisively to enable the uniform electoral procedure to be put into effect in good time for the fifth elections to the European Parliament in 1999;

Instructs its President to forward these proposals to the Council, the Commission, the parliaments and governments of the Member States.

---

1. This proposal has been drafted by Karel De Gucht and Andrew Duff.
2. *Panachage* means that each elector has a certain number of votes — in this case we suggest four — to distribute between either one or several of the candidates.

ANNEX THREE

PROPOSAL FOR A SIMPLIFIED CO-DECISION PROCEDURE
(ARTICLE 189b)

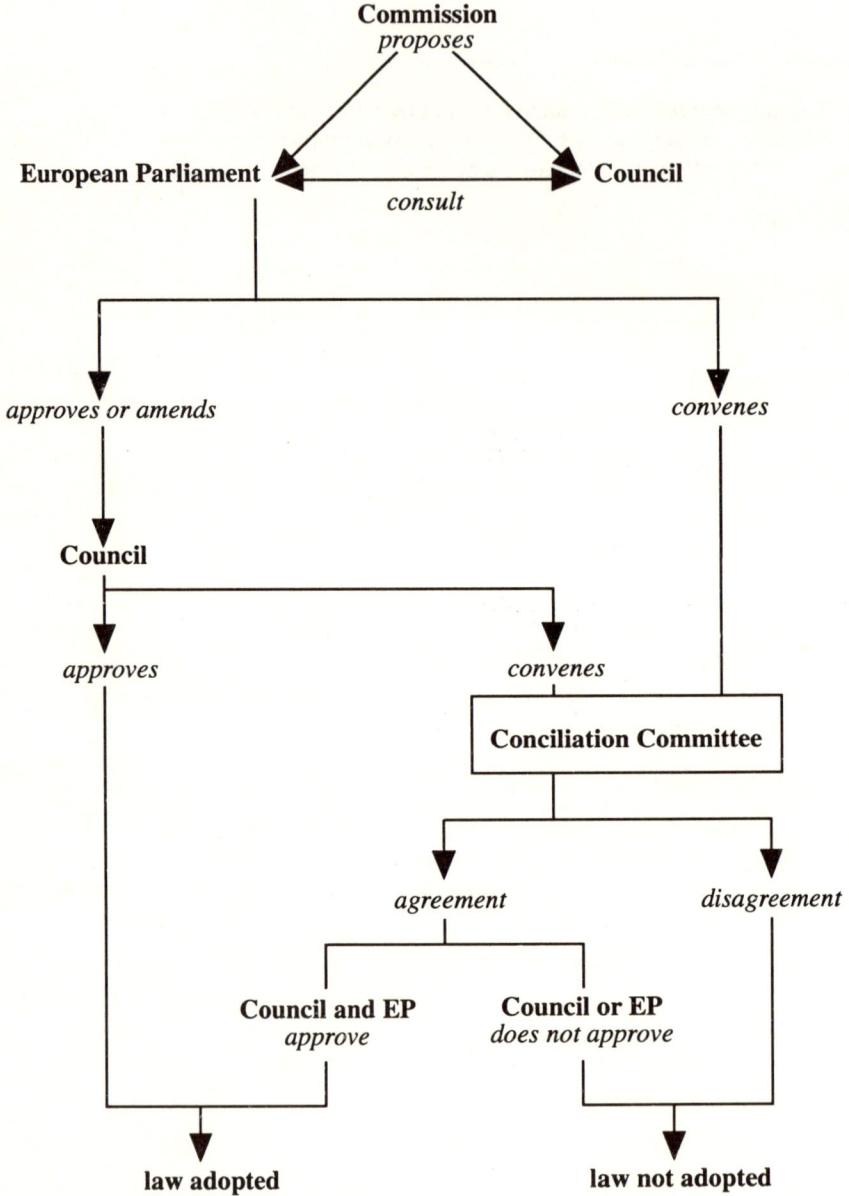